HER MAJESTY QUEEN ELIZABETH II

THE CORONATION SERVICE

Its Meaning and History

BY

FRANCIS C. EELES
O.B.E., D.LITT., LL.D.

LONDON
A. R. MOWBRAY & Co. LIMITED

First published in 1952
Second impression, 1953

PRINTED IN GREAT BRITAIN BY
A. R. MOWBRAY & CO. LIMITED IN THE CITY OF OXFORD
357

PREFACE

THE writer disclaims all originality. He has only attempted to gather from well-known sources the information required by any one who wishes to know a little about the Coronation Service, its meaning and its history, and all the interesting and unusual things that are done in the course of it.

There have been many different coronation services. Here in England there are some half a dozen variant forms. In recent years much study has been given to them. All the English ones are now accessible in print and edited by competent scholars.

The latest contribution to the subject is an excellent picture book entitled *The Historic Story of the Coronation*, by Mr. Lawrence Tanner, M.V.O., F.S.A., Keeper of the Muniments of Westminster Abbey. It gives a far better general idea of the ceremonial than any series of rubrics.

Another fairly recent book is *A History of the English Coronation*, by P. E. Schramm, rather more constitutional than liturgical, but of the first importance.

For the student within reach of a good library, the most generally useful book is still *English Coronation Records*, by L. G. Wickham Legg, London, 1901, full of important documents and

3

with the most significant of them translated into English.

A word of caution. While the service for the last coronation has been reprinted here, it should be borne in mind that no one knows yet, or may know for some time, the exact details of the service as it will be used for the Queen, inasmuch as small variations have frequently been made for different sovereigns.

Attention should be drawn here to a very important tract issued by the Church Historical Society many years ago, called 'Suggestions for the Reconstruction of the Coronation Ceremonies,' by L. G. Wickham Legg, S.P.C.K., 1902. This contains suggestions for the correction of unfortunate alterations made in the service in comparatively recent times.

The Appendix contains the modern service as used for the late King George VI, and also an account, with the most important sections in full, of the service in its longest developed form, which came down unchanged from Edward II's coronation in 1308 until it was abridged and mutilated for James II in 1685. This form of the service is of very great length and too long to reproduce in full in the space available here.[1] The writer does not claim that this version is wholly satisfactory.

---

[1] It should be pointed out that this book is historical and descriptive and no attempt has been made to criticize or suggest alterations.

CONTENTS

LIST OF ILLUSTRATIONS

THE CORONATION SERVICE

Chapter I

THE CONSECRATION OF THE KING

THERE is nothing else now in the world like our Coronation Service. Similar rites once used in other countries have long gone out of use. But the English Coronation Service remains, still full of vitality, and still cherished by the peoples of the British Commonwealth, even by those who know nothing of its contents, their meaning or their history. It is necessarily a service of great elaboration, full of observances that have accumulated from time to time down the ages, protected and preserved by the innate distrust of change that surrounds the deeper things which are at the heart of the national consciousness.

This long and elaborate service with all its external splendour, in its most fully developed form, came down from the time of Edward II, 1308, through the Reformation period unchanged, till the time of James II in 1685, save that it was used in an English translation for James I, Charles I, and Charles II, and that the Communion Service in the Prayer Book took the place of the Latin rite.

In 1685 there were some unfortunate alterations

9

caused by James II being a Roman Catholic and refusing to receive Holy Communion in the Church of England. Some of these mistakes were corrected at the next coronation, that of William of Orange and Mary II, and in this form the service came down through the eighteenth and nineteenth centuries to the present day. In all its essentials, and in much beside, it is true to say that the same service was used for King George VI as had been used for the Saxon kings before the Normans came here.

The Coronation Service is no mere blessing of the King at the beginning of his reign, nor is it merely an impressive religious ceremony to grace an important national occasion. It is much more. It is intended to be the consecration of the sovereign to a definitely ecclesiastical position carried out with great stateliness and elaboration.

THE GENERAL SIGNIFICATION OF THE SERVICE

Before we can go into the details of the various parts of it, and their history and meaning, we must try to see the service as a whole and explain what its compilers intended it to signify. As already indicated, we are not concerned here with what is desirable or otherwise, but with the views actually expressed by the service itself. These we shall try to explain.

First of all we note that the service is called the Consecration of the King, *consecratio regis*, and that the intention is to consecrate the sovereign as a minister of the Church, set apart for special obligations, and that the actual crowning is secondary to this.

We shall find some startling things, forgotten by many people to-day, who have never had to consider the question of the relation of the sovereign to Church and State, either in its historical or in its practical aspect. We have to face the conception which runs through the Coronation Service and was familiar in many areas of Christendom of old, that the King is no mere lay person, but is to be regarded as one of the clergy, though at the same time not a priest.

OLD TESTAMENT PRECEDENTS

The mediaeval liturgists were greatly impressed by Scriptural precedents, and they found many references to the anointing of kings and their religious character in the Old Testament. It was said of the King Melchizedech that he was the priest of the most high God.[1] The anointing of kings at the beginning of their reigns is spoken of in the Book of Judges, in Jotham's parable of the trees going forth to anoint a king over them,[2] ascribed by some to the time of Samuel. Possibly earlier than any of these is the use of oil on the stone set up as a pillar by Jacob at Bethel.[3] Then there are the anointing of the Tabernacle and its furniture[4] and that of Saul,[5] David,[6] and Solomon.[7]

[1] Gen. xiv. 18.   [2] Judges ix. 7–15.   [3] Gen. xxviii. 18.
[4] Exodus xxx. 25.   [5] 1 Sam. x. 1.   [6] ibid., xvi. 13.
[7] 1 Kings i. 39–40.

Elijah was commanded to anoint Elisha to be prophet in his place, as well as the two kings Hazael and Jehu.[1] When David reproved the Amalekite who had killed Saul, it was for destroying one whose person was sacred in virtue of the unction he had received.[2] S. Augustine, commenting on this very passage, calls the royal unction a sacrament. We note that at this time and for long after there was no rigid list of seven sacraments, but the word was used for many symbolic services.[3]

In the Christian Church, as soon as persecution ceased, we find the King holding much the same ecclesiastical position as he did under the older dispensation. This is a matter about which the practice of primitive times can tell us nothing, for during the first few centuries of the Christian era kings were the open and avowed enemies of the Church: yet even at that time we find S. Paul, in the Epistle to the Romans, insisting that the King is the 'minister of God,' not merely as 'a revenger to execute wrath,' but also 'for good.'[4]

---

[1] 1 Kings xix. 15–16.   [2] 2 Sam. i. 14.

[3] See the late Fr. Puller, S.S.J.E., *The Anointing of the Sick and the numbering of the Sacraments*, Church Historical Society, No. 77, where Fr. Puller points out that the limitation to seven is not found until Peter Lombard about the middle of the twelfth century.

[4] Rom. xiii. 4.

Chapter II

THE ENGLISH CORONATION

IN these islands the rite of Sacring, or Consecration, of Kings goes back to the time of S. Columba, who, we are told, blessed Aidan, King of Dalriada, with the laying on of hands on the island of Iona in A.D. 574. When the rite of unction was first used in this connection in the Christian Church is not known; but it must certainly have been in use long before the eighth century, when we find it provided for in the Coronation Service in the Pontifical of Archbishop Egbert of York, 732–766.

THE CORONATION ORDER COMPARED WITH THAT FOR CONSECRATING A BISHOP

To show the way in which the King was anciently regarded by the Church, we may compare the English mediaeval services for the Consecration of a King with those for the Consecration of a Bishop. Consecration was, as we have seen, the old name for the Coronation Service. Here are outlines of the two services side by side:

CONSECRATION OF A BISHOP	CONSECRATION OF THE KING
Oath of obedience to the Metropolitan See, and examination by the Archbishop.	Oath to observe the laws of S. Edward, and instruction by the Archbishop.
Litany, laying on of hands, and *Veni Creator*.	*Veni Creator*, Litany, and, anciently perhaps, laying on of hands.
Collect.	Four Collects.
Consecratory Preface (like that in the Eucharist).	Consecrating Preface (like that in the Eucharist).
Anointing.	Anointing.
	Vesting with albe, dalmatic, and stole.
Delivery of crozier, ring, and mitre, with the book of the Gospels.	Girding with sword; delivery of *pallium regale*, crown, ring, sceptre, and rod.
Eucharist.	Eucharist.

The vestments worn by the King are all ecclesiastical. An old account of the Coronation of Henry VI of England says:

'They arrayed him like as a bishop that should sing Mass, with a dalmatic like a tunic, and a stole about his neck but not crossed, and sandalled, and also with hosen and shoes and cope and gloves like a bishop.'[1]

In the form for the Consecration of the King, the archbishop used to pray that the King may

[1] Brit. Mus. MS. Nero, c. ix, ff. 172*b*, and 173.

'nourish and teach, defend and instruct' the Church and people. This form came down from Anglo-Saxon times to those of William and Mary in 1689, when it was omitted.

Outside England it is much the same. In one of the prayers in the Imperial Coronation Service in the older Roman Pontificals, the Holy Roman Emperor is spoken of as ruling the Church; this is found as late as 1542. The same Pontifical (1542) directs that the emperor is to be received by the Canons of S. Peter's vested in a surplice and a grey furred almuce[1] like one of themselves; and at the offertory the rubric directs that the emperor shall offer the chalice and paten with hosts in the place of the sub-deacon, together with the water for the mixture.

In another Imperial Coronation Order the rubric says:

'They vest him in amice, albe, and girdle. And so they bring him to the Lord Pope . . . and he makes him a clergyman; and gives him the tunic, dalmatic, and cope and mitre, the buskins and sandals.'

The emperor had also the right to read or sing the Gospel at Mass, the King of France or the King of Sicily reading the Epistle. In 1414, at Constance,

---

[1] The almuce was a furred cape with a hood behind and two tails or pendants in front, worn over the surplice in choir by canons and dignitaries. It is sometimes called an amess, but must not be confused with the amice, one of the eucharistic vestments, a linen cloth worn on the head or neck with a large embroidered band like a collar, called an apparel.

Kings were sometimes made canons of cathedrals. A stall in St. David's is reserved to the Crown of England, and the King of Scotland was a Canon of Glasgow, with a stall in choir, and a place or voice and a vote in Chapter (Robertson, *Concilia Scotiae*, i, p. cxx).

the Emperor Sigismund read the Gospel of the first
Mass of Christmas Day at the Papal Mass, vested
like a deacon.

Of course, both royal and ecclesiastical vestments
are ultimately of secular origin.

MEDIAEVAL TEACHING ABOUT THE KING

Lyndewode, the great English canonist, commenting upon the King's power of instituting to
the deanery of S. Martin-le-Grand, London, quotes
the view that 'the anointed King is not a mere lay
person, but one of mixed character,'[1] though he does
not accept it himself, and he goes on to quote another
writer, who says that the King of England 'is the
lord of all the Churches of England and Normandy.'
Another well-known canonist, Henry de Bartholo-
maeis, Cardinal of Ostia, commonly known as
Hostiensis, says that the royal unction confers
grace on the King for the office he is called upon to
exercise;[2] and Robert Grosseteste, Bishop of Lincoln,
1235–1254, explains that grace as being the seven-
fold gifts of the Holy Ghost.[3] Henry de Bracton,
the great English lawyer of the thirteenth century,
only repeats the teaching of the Church in Anglo-
Saxon times when he calls the King God's vicar
upon earth,[4] for the laws of S. Edward, to which

---

[1] Lyndewode, *Provinciale*, l, iii; tit. *De cohabitatione clericorum*; cap.
Ut clericalis; verb. *beneficiati*.

[2] *Summa Aurea*, l, i, de sacra unctione, Lyons, 1548, fo. 35*b*.

[3] *Roberti Grosseteste episcopi quondam Lincolniensis epistolae*, Rolls Series,
1861, p. 350.

[4] H. de Bracton, *De legibus et consuetudinibus Angliae*, Rolls Series,
1878, i, p. 38, ii, p. 172, v, 402.

THE ENTHRONEMENT
Coronation of George VI

the English kings promised obedience, laid down that 'the King is the Vicar of the Great King [*vicarius summi regis*] to rule the kingdom and people of the Lord, and, above all, Holy Church, and to defend it and them from all who would harm them.'[1]

Quite late in the Middle Ages an Archbishop of Reims addressed King Charles VII thus:

'You, my sovereign Lord, are not merely a lay person, but an Ecclesiastical Prelate, the first in your Kingdom, and after the Pope, the right arm of the Church.'

It would be possible to quote similar passages from other French churchmen of repute.

When doctrine such as this was taught not only by canonists and theologians, but by the services of the Church themselves, it is not wonderful that, in the reaction against papal domination in England, Henry VIII was styled Supreme Head of the Church. This grossly exaggerated title was afterwards given up and was not resumed by Elizabeth,[2] although Queen Mary did not think the use of it inconsistent with loyalty to the pope, and actually granted a licence to preach.[3]

It is important to notice that the teaching about the King which was current in Tudor times was not an invention but an exaggeration.

---

[1] Thorpe, *Ancient Laws*, London, 1840, p. 193.

[2] But one of the seals of George III, in use for a few years, has it (A. B. and A. Wyon, *Great Seals of England*, London, 1887, p. 127).

[3] Collier, *Records*, num. lxviii; repeated *Ecclesiastical History*, vol. ix, p. 300; reprinted by W. E. Collins, *The English Reformation*, London, 1891, Appendix iii, p. 226.

B

· THE KING AND THE STATE

The rise of Ultramontanism — the extreme development of the Roman doctrine as to the position of the pope—has naturally brought with it a practical denial of the Church's ancient doctrine about the King and his position. A like result has also been produced by that denial of so much of the sacramental system of the Church which has spread over these islands in various forms during the last three hundred years. And the strong development of another doctrine regarding the King—namely, that of Divine Right—has also done much to obscure the old teaching. The way in which the regal power has been abused—sometimes used against the Church—made men forget the other use of it. But what is more responsible than anything for the present state of feeling in the matter is that most people confuse the King with the State. With an older—and, to our way of thinking, a more satisfactory—constitution, the State was Christian, and the King was identified with it in practice in a way that he is not now. Forgetful of this, many people of our day mistake the ancient Catholic teaching as to the King for a statement of Erastian heresy, and with disastrous results. Erastianism is a theory of Church government which subjects the Church to an external force—the State, a minister, a public officer, or the House of Commons. It is not the acknowledgement of the position held by the King in virtue of his anointing and consecration to an office within the Church. The two ideas are different, if not antagonistic. No one would accuse the late Bishop Gore of a desire to keep the Church in bondage to the State. 'Erastianism,' he says, 'is a name which describes the parody of an ideal which is in itself noble, and deep-rooted in the ancient traditions of the Church and nation.'[1] Erastianism is a very different thing from what Dr. Church, once Dean of S. Paul's, called the visitatorial power of the crown: 'the right claimed by the Crown as a divine power, to see that the Church, also a divine power and institution, does the work appointed her by God: and to interfere if she does not.'[2] On the other hand, it must of course be borne in mind that, in the words of Article XXXVII, 'we give not to our Princes the ministering either of God's Word, or of the Sacraments.' No really priest-like functions ever seem to have been performed by the King of England.

It may well be pointed out that the teaching of the service here given is also the teaching of the East as well as of the West. In the Russian Church on Orthodoxy Sunday (the First Sunday in Lent) some notable heretics are abjured, and among them those 'who say that Orthodox Princes do not ascend their thrones by the special grace of God, and do not

[1] *Guardian*, February 19, 1896, p. 271.
[2] On the Relations between Church and State, in *Christian Remembrancer*, April, 1850: reprinted by Macmillan, 1899, p. 17.

at their unction receive the gift of the Holy Ghost for the discharge of their great office.'[1]

PRAYERS FOR THE KING

The relation of the King to the Church is also shown by the special way in which he is prayed for. These frequent prayers in the Prayer Book have sometimes been criticized by those who have never come across the large amount of precedent and authority which exists for them.

The Collect for the King in the Communion Service has ample authority outside the Prayer Book.[2] A thirteenth-century General Synod of the Church of Scotland passed a Canon to the effect that a collect for the King and Queen and their children should be said in every Mass except on great festivals.

The prayers added to Mattins and Evensong in 1662 have excellent English precedent. In the tenth and eleventh centuries, after each of the canonical hours, two psalms were said, one for the King, the other for the King, Queen, and Royal Family, with certain prayers for them.

The versicle, 'O Lord, save the King,' with its response, was translated direct from the old divine service of the Sarum Breviary when it was reformed in the sixteenth century. It is in all Western Breviaries; and it remains in the present-day Roman Breviary.

[1] J. M. Neale, *History of the Holy Eastern Church*, pt. i, p. 875.
[2] Though, of course, it was a mistake to place it before the other collects, as was done in 1662.

The Leofric Missal and that of Robert of Jumièges, to mention only English instances, give a daily Mass for the King, of which the present collect takes the place.

In a Roman Missal, with Portuguese proper offices, printed at Lisbon in 1784, a collect for the King, Queen, and Royal Family is ordered in the form of a long addition to the Collect for the Day. And in 1857, at the request of Napoleon III, Pius IX expressly allowed '*Et pro Imperatore nostro*, N' ('And for our Emperor so-and-so') to be added in the canon of the Mass throughout France, with a versicle and response for the emperor after the Communion, and a post-Communion for him, besides a solemn collect on Good Friday, a clause in the Paschal Praeconium on Easter Eve, and no less than three petitions and prayers in the Litany of the Saints.

Having seen something of the theological background of the relation of Kings to the Church, we are in a position to consider the Coronation Service itself. As in the case of the Eucharist, as with Baptism and the other rites of the Church, certain things must everywhere and always be done, but the way of doing them varies in different places. There is no one form of Coronation Service received throughout the Church, any more than there is one Eucharistic liturgy. Within certain well-defined limits the Coronation Service varies in different places, just as we find different liturgies and uses. As the Thirty-fourth Article says: 'Every particular or national Church hath authority to ordain, change, and abolish, ceremonies or rites of the Church ordained only by man's authority.'

In the short space at our disposal it is impossible to do otherwise than confine our attention to the English Coronation Service and its several varieties. They are good representatives of what such services have been. The King of England has always ranked high among European kings. There were something like thirty princes in early mediaeval Europe who called themselves kings, but until a comparatively late period only some four besides the Holy Roman Emperor were crowned or anointed. These were the Kings of England, France, Sicily, and Jerusalem. Two of them had the peculiar privilege of unction with a compound oil of a specially sacred character over and above the ordinary royal unction, and they were the Kings of England and France.

THE VARIOUS FORMS OF THE ENGLISH SERVICE

The English Coronation Service is much the same as it was in the eighth century—more than a thousand years ago. There are, however, some seven different forms of it, two of which are almost identical. These may be divided into two groups— Latin and English. There are four different varieties of the Latin order—all older than the middle of the fourteenth century, when the service may be said to have attained a state of completion, in which it remained until late in the seventeenth century.

For it is important to notice that the Coronation Service was practically untouched by the Reformation. The same Latin service was used for Elizabeth as for Henry VII and Henry VIII. It was translated into English for James I (VI of Scotland), and thus the fourth and most perfect of the Latin forms of the service may be accounted the first English form, for liturgically they are almost identical. A full description with the most significant parts of the service at its fullest will be found in Appendix I. It does not seem worth while to overburden this short sketch with a long description of the earlier forms of the Latin service; they seem to have passed out of use before the fourteenth century. Enough to say that in the earliest of them—in the MS. Pontifical of Archbishop Egbert of York, 732–766—the Coronation Service is inserted in the Communion Service after the Gospel—in exactly the same way as the Consecration of a Bishop;[1] and the actual crowning took place last of all, instead of before the delivery of the sceptres. In the subsequent forms of the service—that is, in the later Saxon and the Norman ones, and also in the Liber Regalis and the Stewart orders—until the end of the seventeenth century, the Coronation Order precedes the Mass.

[1] After the Gospel is liturgically the same place in the service as after the Creed, which had not been introduced into the Latin Mass in Archbishop Egbert's time. Either place corresponds roughly to the division between the Mass of the Catechumens and the Mass of the Faithful, although the Creed properly belongs to the latter.

THE JAMES II AND SUBSEQUENT ORDERS

The second English order stands by itself: it is that used for James II. As we have already said, he was a Romanist, and refused to receive Communion; the service was therefore altered so as to get rid of the celebration of the Eucharist, for at a rite celebrated by the clergy of the Church of England it was impossible that a Roman Catholic could communicate—even for the reception of unction at their hands it was thought advisable to get permission from the Roman Court. Changes thus became necessary, and to conceal the real motive for the change, the plea was put forward that the Coronation Service was too long. The Archbishop of Canterbury (Dr. Sancroft) was directed to shorten it, keeping to essentials; but he rode on the top of his commission and did very much more, altering most of the prayers in accordance with the debased liturgical taste of the day. When William and Mary came in 1689 the service underwent further changes, not all for the better, although much of the mischief done for James II was repaired. The Communion Service was restored, and the Coronation Service, instead of preceding it, was inserted in the middle, in the position it occupied in the earliest order of all—that of Egbert. A return was made to earlier custom in some details of the anointing; the crown was delivered last, as in Egbert's Pontifical, and the form for blessing the oil was considerably strengthened. This William and Mary recension came down

THE CROWNING
Coronation of George VI

through the eighteenth century, and was used for the Coronation of Queen Victoria in 1838, and then again in our own time for Edward VII, 1902, George V, 1911, and for our late King, George VI, in 1937. In its latest form it is given here. A few little things dropped out one by one, chiefly through negligence in Georgian times; for no one understood the service, and few cared about it. It is really wonderful that it survived in such a full and elaborate form as it has. But it must be clearly understood that, setting aside the James II order, which was never used again, the alterations and omissions had little or no doctrinal signification; they were the result of a craze for shortening the service, coupled with ignorance, bad liturgical taste, and great carelessness. There was no need for doctrinal change; the old mediaeval service passed through the Reformation unaltered; not, as it were, by accident, for when translated for James I no real change was made, and the same service that was used for Edward II was used for Charles II. And even taking into account the alterations made at the end of the seventeenth century, the Coronation Service used for the late King is remarkably like that used for all his predecessors. As a work of liturgical art, those alterations spoiled it greatly, but they in no way changed its theological character, and they were all omissions of what have never been regarded as essentials in any part of the Church.

Chapter III

THE CORONATION SERVICE

SOME of the Saxon kings were crowned at Kingston-on-Thames, about ten miles southwest of London, others at Winchester, and one, Edgar, at Bath; but since the time of S. Edward the Confessor the Coronation has usually taken place in the Abbey Church of S. Peter at Westminster, not in Canterbury or any other cathedral, and not in any of the Chapels Royal. And if we look beyond England we find that crowning places have more often been collegiate than cathedral churches: S. Peter's at Rome, where the emperor used to be crowned, is not a cathedral church; the Church of S. Ambrose, and not the metropolitan church, was the crowning place at Milan; S. Petronius, and not the cathedral, at Bologna; Aachen was only a cathedral for a few years in quite modern times. Scone and Holyrood, not St. Andrews or any other cathedral, were the coronation places in Scotland. But the King of France was crowned in Reims Cathedral, and the Danish King of England, Canute, was crowned in S. Paul's, London.

As with the Consecration of a Bishop, a coronation was anciently ordered to take place on a Sunday or holy day. Queen Victoria was crowned on the eve of S. Peter, the patron saint of Westminster

Abbey. The Holy Roman Emperor was supposed to be crowned on Mid-Lent Sunday.

THE PRESENT SERVICE IN DETAIL

It will perhaps be as well to choose for our detailed description the Coronation Order used for King George VI in 1937, here reprinted in Appendix II, adding a few words of explanation where they seem to be needed.

The first rubric is as follows:

'In the morning upon the day of the Coronation early, care is to be taken that the Ampulla be filled with Oil and, together with the Spoon, be laid ready upon the Altar in the Abbey Church.'

The ampulla is a golden vessel for the holy oil, shaped like an eagle with outstretched wings. It is about nine inches high. Through the beak the Archbishop of Canterbury pours some of the oil into the spoon, with which he anoints the Sovereign. The use of the word altar may be noted, and it has continued all through the eighteenth and nineteenth centuries down to the present day in the Coronation Service, as indeed elsewhere.

Much of the traditional arrangement of the altar in Westminster Abbey came down to the nineteenth century as we see from pictures of the coronation of Queen Victoria.

The main structure of the screen against which the altar stands is mediaeval, including the two doorways, one on either side, leading into

S. Edward's Chapel behind, where the shrine and its altar are situated.

The reredos and decorations on the west side of the screen date from the nineteenth-century restoration by Sir Gilbert Scott, whose reconstruction is in general not far from what the drawing in the Islip Roll shows the altar to have been at the end of the mediaeval period. Recent improvements have gone further to restore the old arrangement.

The use of the magnificent plate for decoration instead of flowers has always been the practice at coronations though not confined to them. It was the ancient custom generally at feasts, and may still be seen in other great churches like Chichester, or Salisbury, Exeter, Lincoln, or Durham.

THE PROCESSION

Until the time of George IV those who were to take part in the coronation assembled in Westminster Hall and went from thence in solemn procession to the Abbey Church. This was a liturgical procession, and in it were carried the chalice and paten as well as the regalia. Incense also was used in it and flowers scattered as late as 1685. At least since the Coronation of Richard I, in 1189, three swords have been borne before the King in this procession: the Sword of Mercy with the blunt point (called Curtana), the Sword of Justice to the Clergy on the right, that of Justice to the Temporality on the left.

THE RECOGNITION

Between the choir and the altar of the Abbey Church a raised platform is prepared, called the theatre. In the centre the throne is placed. Before the altar is the ancient Chair of S. Edward, with the Stone of Destiny, which was brought from Scone, below it. Between it and the throne is a lesser chair and a folding stool, or faldstool, at which one could either kneel or sit.

On arrival at the stage or 'theatre' set up in the centre of the crossing in the Abbey Church, the Sovereign bows to the altar and stands in the south side for what is called the Recognition. For this the Archbishop and some high officers of State present the new monarch for the approval of the people and go to the parts of the theatre facing east, south, west, and north, saying:

'Sirs, I here present unto you King George, your undoubted King: Wherefore all you who are come this day to do your homage and service, Are you willing to do the same?'

Meanwhile the King turns himself, following the movements of the Archbishop.

The answer is prolonged applause.

This ceremony is a relic of popular election which must have come down from remote times, and is believed to be of Teutonic origin.

After the Recognition, the regalia which have been carried in procession are set on the altar.

The Archbishop puts on his cope—a survival of the old ceremonial vesting at the altar.

Then the Sovereign kneels before the altar and makes the First Oblation, offering an altar frontal and an ingot of gold of a pound weight which the Archbishop receives and places reverently on the altar, saying the prayer, 'O God, who dwellest,' etc.

THE OATH

Next comes the Oath. This is the Coronation Oath, properly so called. It is true that a Declaration against certain Roman doctrines was made in some coronations—those of Anne and the earlier Georges; but it has been made before Parliament and not in the service at all since George IV.

The Coronation Oath is of great antiquity: the Declaration was only made in 1702 with a view to excluding a Romanist from the throne—a thing it would be powerless to do in the case of a really unscrupulous king, in spite of its violent language. It forms no part of the service, and we need not discuss it here: enough to point out that a plain statement that the Sovereign is not a Roman Catholic, or that he is a member of the Church of England, would be quite sufficient to serve the purpose in the case of an honest man, and in the case of one who is dishonest, no form of words could be invented that would be sufficient to prevent all subterfuges!

Its wording has varied slightly: the last form of it will be found on p. 66.

In most of the old orders the coronation was at once proceeded with, but in the earliest form of all, and again at and since the coronation of William and Mary, the Coronation Service has been placed, like the consecration of a bishop, between the two parts of the Communion Service, the *missa catechumenorum* and the *missa fidelium*; that is, immediately before the offertory.

The Archbishop is, of course, the celebrant, and the rubric directs the Epistle to be read by one bishop, and the Gospel by another, following the ancient English custom on great occasions.

THE ANOINTING

After the Creed follows the anointing, with the hymn '*Veni, Creator*' and the blessing of the oil. In the earlier orders this was preceded by the Litany and certain consecratory prayers. In the post-Revolution orders, the Litany and one of these prayers come at an earlier part of the service. At the last coronation the Litany was omitted here, having been sung in procession when the Dean and Chapter of Westminster went from the altar to the west end to meet the Royal Party with the Archbishop.

In the Latin rite on Maundy Thursday three different oils were blessed by the bishop. The oil of the sick and the oil of catechumens were of simple olive oil: the third, the cream, or chrism, was a compound oil, made with olive oil and balm. It was the most important and holy of the three, and was used for Confirmation, Ordination of Priests, and Consecration of Bishops, and was thus considered a special vehicle for the communication of the Holy Spirit. At the present day, in some foreign churches, a lamp is kept burning before the place where the cream is kept. This oil was used in addition to the ordinary holy oil, or oil of catechumens, in the case of the Kings of England and France—a privilege not enjoyed by the Holy Roman Emperor. In the fourteenth century the anointing took place as follows: First the King's hands were anointed, then his breast, back, shoulders, and elbows, and a cross was made upon his head, all with the ordinary holy oil, and finally a second cross was made on his head with the cream.

The Stewart Kings after the Reformation were anointed with a very elaborate compound oil, made of some nine ingredients, which was blessed at a special service early on the day of the coronation. It resembled in its many constituents the oil used for the anointing of the Emperor of Russia—a special oil used in the Russian Church for Confirmation, with about thirty or forty ingredients. Since the time of William and Mary the oil has been blessed during the service, just before the anointing. Until Charles II's time a Preface like that in the Eucharist, with 'Lift up your hearts,' etc., and 'It is very meet, right,' etc.,

THE PROCESSION FROM THE ABBEY
Coronation of George VI

was said here:[1] but since 1838 the '*Veni, Creator*' has been followed at once by the prayer:

'O Lord, Holy Father, who by anointing with Oil didst of old make and consecrate kings, priests, and prophets, to teach and govern thy people Israel: Bless and sanctify thy chosen servant GEORGE, who by our office and ministry is now to be anointed with this Oil, [*Here the Archbishop is to lay his hand upon the Ampulla.*] and consecrated King: Strengthen him, O Lord, with the Holy Ghost the Comforter: confirm and stablish him with thy free and princely Spirit, the Spirit of wisdom and government, the Spirit of counsel and ghostly strength, the Spirit of knowledge and true godliness, and fill him, O Lord, with the Spirit of thy holy fear, now and for ever. *Amen.*'

This is expressed in far stronger language than it was in mediaeval times, or in the days of Charles I. And this prayer has been in use by the English Sovereigns since the Revolution period of 1689, a time at which it might have been expected that no very distinct views of the sacred character of the Sovereign would be expressed. This, it is plain, sets forth that the King is consecrated: and consecrated 'by our office and ministry'; that is, by the hands of the Archbishop of Canterbury. It is impossible in the presence of this prayer to assert, as the writer has heard it asserted, with any show of speaking the truth, that the Kings of England,

[1] The omission of this Preface was a great mistake: such a formula has been so widely accepted as the solemn beginning of especially important petitions and consecrations.

C

at all events since the Revolution of 1689, 'neither asked for nor expected supernatural graces in their Coronation and Anointing.'

THE VESTMENTS

Then comes the delivery of the vestments and ornaments. Before the time of James II the rubrics directed the use of each, and some were blessed. Latterly some of these forms have been omitted, although all the vestments and ornaments have been used. The earlier use regarding them will be found in Appendix I.

There is some trace of the use of the amice in a kind of linen cap sometimes used, but generally speaking the first is the colobium sindonis, a linen vestment, a form of albe, almost exactly like it, if it has sleeves; like the sleeveless rochet, if it has none. Latterly this vestment became very much degraded— as indeed did most of the Royal vestments—losing its sleeves after Charles II, and being somewhat cut down and trimmed with lace, its original form and ecclesiastical character being thereby taken from it. In the case of Queen Victoria it was cut low in the neck and split up the sides.

Next is delivered the supertunica, a silk vestment, exactly like a tunicle or dalmatic. Latterly this vestment has been divided up the front like an early nineteenth-century surplice.

Here follows the delivery of the spurs and the oblation and girding of the sword.

Then comes the armill, or stole. It was put

round the neck, and the ends were tied so as to hang from each elbow, and it thus partook also of the nature of a maniple or fanon, or rather of two maniples. In the West, both in the Roman and the other similar rites, it is usual for the stole to be put on immediately after the albe or surplice; but at Milan in the Ambrosian rite the deacon wears the stole over the dalmatic. This is also done in the Eastern Church in Greece and Russia. In some parts of the East there are two cuff-like vestments corresponding to the maniple: one is used on each arm; and in the tying of the armill to the elbows we may perhaps see a trace of something similar. In the case of Queen Victoria and subsequently the armill was not tied to the elbows, but was allowed to hang straight down, like a bishop's stole. It was not worn like a deacon's stole, as some have thought. In her case, and in that of Charles II, the armill was ornamented with crosses—an innovation on English practice, which was not to put crosses on stoles, although they were often used on chasubles. Anciently bracelets were also delivered, and it is possible that the ends of the stole were at one time tied to them.

Then comes the pallium regale, or imperial robe, corresponding to the cope or chasuble. Anciently made like a chasuble, it has latterly been made very nearly like a cope. The chasuble and cope, it must be noted, are really different forms of the same vestment and are sometimes interchanged. At Eichstadt at the present day a form of chasuble is said to be in use which is divided on one side and is put on like a cope and not over the head. The principal Armenian Eucharistic vestment is exactly like a cope. The pallium regale is embroidered all over with golden eagles, symbolical of the Sovereign's imperial authority as overlord in Britain.

THE ORNAMENTS

Since James II's time the orb has been delivered here, owing to a misunderstanding of its real nature.

After the delivery of the vestments comes the investiture, *per annulum et baculum*, as it is called, or delivery of the ring and sceptre.

The ring is like a bishop's, and is a ruby or sapphire inlaid with a cross. It is delivered with the following form and placed on the fourth finger of the right hand, where the wedding ring was placed before 1549, and where it is still placed according to most foreign rites at the present day:

'Receive this Ring, the ensign of kingly dignity, and of defence of the Catholic Faith.'

The Sovereign has already professed belief in the Catholic Faith by reciting the Nicene Creed and by repeating the words, 'I believe one Catholic and Apostolic Church.' This and the description of the ring as the seal of the Catholic Faith formed part of the service long before the words 'Protestant Reformed Religion established by Law' were added to the oath, and they were not altered at that time. It is clear, then—setting everything else on one side—that the 'Protestant Reformed Religion established by Law' can only be interpreted in a sense agreeable to the rest of the service; namely, as indicating the Church of England as the Catholic Church as opposed to the Roman Church in the country, not as any and every form of religion that calls itself Protestant.

The oath in the Coronation Service has no relation to Scotland. The King takes the oath relating to the security of the Presbyterian Church of Scotland before the Privy Council, and not in the Coronation Service, and that oath concerns only Scotland, as the other concerns only England.

The delivery of the ring is followed by that of the gloves—another episcopal ornament.

Here followed the Crowning in all the more ancient English orders, except that in Egbert's Pontifical: but since the time of William and Mary the delivery of the sceptres has preceded it.

There are two sceptres, according to the English custom. The first, placed in the King's right hand, is the sceptre proper, and has a ball at one end and a cross at the other. The second, held in the left hand, is surmounted by a dove, and is sometimes called the rod. The first is 'the ensign of kingly power and justice,' the second 'of equity and mercy.' The delivery of the orb has already been mentioned. It was at once taken back to the altar.

The orb with the cross is really the same as the sceptre with the cross: it is a shorter form of it, and was sometimes used instead of it. Unfortunately, Archbishop Sancroft seems to have mistaken it for a different ornament, and delivered it separately in consequence. If it is used at all, precedent requires that it should take the place of the first sceptre, which it really is.

Then comes the putting on of the crown by the Archbishop.

Anciently it was placed on the altar, blessed, and censed.

The forms used at the blessing and delivery of all these ornaments have varied to a large extent, and although all survived until the time of Charles II, many were omitted in the later orders.

Last of all comes the delivery of the Bible, a new ceremony introduced in the case of William and Mary, but one which happens closely to correspond to the delivery of the Gospels to a newly conse-crated bishop.

THE BLESSING AND ENTHRONEMENT

The solemn blessing of the new sovereign now follows. It is long, and of a special character not unlike the blessing in the Marriage Service, and it is immediately followed by a blessing on the congrega-tion. Then comes the inthronization. The sovereign is directed to be lifted up and placed in the throne by the Archbishop, bishops, and other peers of the

kingdom, the Archbishop saying, 'Stand firm, and
hold fast from henceforth the seat and state of royal
and imperial dignity . . .'; a form that has come
down from Saxon times.

FEALTY AND HOMAGE

Then the Lords Spiritual and Temporal do fealty
and homage in the following manner. First the
Archbishop of Canterbury and the rest of the bishops
kneel down before the Sovereign and as their
spokesman he recites the formula of fealty. He then
rises and kisses the King's left cheek. The rest of
the bishops then kiss the King, and the fealty is
done. The Lords Temporal then do homage, kneeling before the Sovereign according to their degrees,
and the premier duke, marquis, earl, and the rest
places his hands between those of the King and
recites the oath of homage. He then, followed by
his fellow peers, touches the crown on the king's
head and kisses his left cheek.

This is the moment at which the coronation of a
queen consort takes place if there be one.

Then follows the rest of the Communion Service.

THE OFFERTORY

At the offertory the King delivers the sceptres
to the Lords who have previously borne them,
descends from the throne and goes to the steps of
the altar, giving up the crown and kneeling.

The rubric directs 'that the King shall offer Bread and Wine for the Communion, which being brought out of Saint Edward's Chapel, and delivered into his hands (the Bread upon the Paten by the Bishop that read the Epistle, and the Wine in the Chalice by the Bishop that read the Gospel), shall by the Archbishop be received from the King, and reverently placed upon the Altar, and decently covered with a fair linen cloth.'

Presumably the paten and chalice with their contents are intended to be prepared before the service. The present rubric goes back to William and Mary. To prepare the chalice before the service was the general practice of old at Low Mass, and still is in the Dominican rite. In the great secular churches, like Sarum, Wells, or Exeter, the preparation at High Mass took place between the Epistle and Gospel. Among the Benedictines it was common for the highest in dignity to receive the elements from the sacrist and then approach the altar, where he placed the bread on the paten held by the celebrant and poured wine into the chalice held by one of the ministers.

The elements having been placed on the altar the Archbishop says the following prayer:

'Bless, O Lord, we beseech thee, these thy gifts, and sanctify them unto this holy use, that by them we may be made partakers of the Body and Blood of thine only-begotten Son Jesus Christ, and fed unto everlasting life of soul and body: And that thy servant King GEORGE may be enabled to the discharge of his weighty office, whereunto of thy great goodness thou hast called and appointed him. Grant this, O Lord, for Jesus Christ's sake, our only Mediator and Advocate. *Amen.*'

This is the collect technically called the Secret, and it has come down from very early times. It is of very high importance because of its doctrinal character. The Coronation Service has passed through the hands of many theologians of divergent views, any one of whom could easily have altered or removed this prayer so as to take away the Catholic teaching as to the Real Presence. But this was not done even when the Declaration against Transubstantiation was introduced in 1702. It is clear, then, that that Declaration cannot be interpreted as condemning the doctrine stated in this collect, but only the perversion of it which those who framed it understood by the term Transubstantiation.

Then the 'second oblation' is made by the King. This has always consisted of a mark of gold. An apparent peculiarity is the offering of it *after* the bread and wine. The Book of Common Prayer and many foreign missals direct that the alms should be offered first and the bread and wine afterwards, the alms being the representative of the older offering of the bread and wine in kind. But the second oblation in the Coronation Service is no such representative of the offering of the elements in kind: it is purely additional, and is therefore made afterwards.

THE COMMUNION

The Archbishop then proceeds with the celebration of the Eucharist, in which a Proper Preface has always been provided. The words have varied at different times.

The King of France, as well as the emperor, had the privilege of Communion in both kinds after the withdrawal of the chalice from the laity; but there is no evidence that the King of England received in both kinds in the later middle ages. The Archbishop of Canterbury, as celebrant, has always administered from the paten to the King. Since the Reformation the chalice has been administered by the Dean of Westminster, seemingly because in the later middle ages the Abbot of Westminster gave the King the wine and water for the purification. The houselling cloth remained in use up to George IV's coronation. The only two Kings of England who did not receive the Holy Communion at their coronation were John and James II, both of more than unhappy memory.

THE END OF THE SERVICE

After the Communion the Sovereign takes the crown and sceptres, returns to the throne to await the end of the service, and afterwards goes into

S. Edward's Chapel, where the coronation ornaments are removed and placed upon the altar.

He then assumes the purple and ermine robe of
State and the rather less heavy imperial crown.

Formerly all returned to Westminster Hall in a
solemn procession like that before the service.

APPENDICES

THE *LIBER REGALIS*

AS we have seen, the Coronation Service reached its fullest form in the rite which has survived in the fourteenth-century manuscript known as the *Liber Regalis*, one of the choicest possessions of Westminster Abbey. In that form it was used for Edward II in 1308 and it came down unchanged through the Reformation, though translated into English for James I.

We will now make an attempt to describe it. As already pointed out, the Coronation Service in the second and third recensions, as they are called, and also in this one, was carried out before the Mass and not within it, at the time of the offertory, as in our earliest Saxon form, an arrangement reverted to in 1689 for William and Mary, and retained ever since.

The service is too long to reproduce in full.

Therefore most of the long prayers are omitted and certain sections, chiefly those still in use, are summarized. Where the forms are given at length the English translation used for Charles I in 1626 has been used as well as in some of the rubrics, though in modern spelling.

The rubrics begin with the preparations in Westminster Abbey, and they go on to describe the ancient procession from Westminster Hall to the Abbey, which began with seating the King on the stone seat—the original 'King's Bench' in the Hall. This ceremony has something in common with the original use of the coronation or rather inauguration stones.

The Apparatus in the Church of Westminster

There is a stage to be set up four square, close to the four high pillars between the quire and the altar: the stage is to be spread with tapestry, and to have rails about it richly covered: it is also to have stairs out of the quire up to it, and down to the altar from it.

There are two thrones of estate to be erected on the said stage: one higher for the King; another lower for the Queen, both adorned with most precious silk covers and cushions, with two chairs before them.

There are also two other chairs to be set below the altar; the one in the south side somewhat higher for the King; the other on the north side, not so high, for the Queen; with either of them a faldstool, and cushions to pray at.

And all the pavement to be spread with carpets.

There is also a traverse to be set up in S. Edward's Chapel, for the King to disrobe himself in, after the ceremonies of his coronation be ended.

The Evening before the Coronation

It is to be provided that the Regalia which are S. Edward's crown, with the residue of the robes, and the oil for the anointing be ready upon the altar.

And that the crowns imperial, and other robes, royal, which the King is to wear (after the rights (*sic*) of his coronation be ended) be brought and laid ready in a traverse, within S. Edward's Chapel.

The Ampulla and Spoon

Liber Regalis

Then are to be delivered to such persons as are appointed to bear them:

1. The regal[1]   4. The long sceptre
2. The paten   5. The rod with the dove
3. The sceptre with the   6. The spurs
   cross

There is also the rayed cloth, to be spread on a floor of boards, from the palace hall door, up to the stage, for his Majesty to tread on all the way.

Which is to be done, and the cloth to be distributed by the heirs of the Lord Beauchampe, Almoner for the coronation day.

A seat in a high place is to be prepared in the Royal Hall, on which the King is raised and from which he proceeds to the church.

THE PROCESSION

and ordering of the Train

The Archbishop and Bishops of the Realm then present, together with the Church and Quire of West-minster, are to meet the King at the Palace Gate in procession wise, singing those things that are wont to be sung at the reception of Kings.

The Lord Chancellor, if he be a Bishop, is to bear the Regal (Chalice) immediately before the King.

Before him the Lord Treasurer, if he be a Bishop, is to bear the Paten.

Otherwise if they be not Bishops that bear those offices his Majesty is to assign two bishops to carry them, such as he likes to name.

[1] S. Edward's agate chalice.

D

Then three Dukes or high nobles are to carry:

1. The sceptre with the cross.
2. The long sceptre.
3. The rod with the dove.

Then the Earls with three swords:

1. The Earl of Chester the curtana.
2. The Earl of Huntingdon the second.
3. The Earl of Warwick the third.

Before them one of the magnates is to carry the spurs.

The King is to go under a canopy of purple silk, borne by the Barons of the Cinque Ports, four of them at every staff.

The King is to be supported by the Bishops of Durham and Bath.

The Abbot or the Dean of Westminster shall always be at the King's side to give him information about those things which concern the solemnity of the Coronation.

The service begins with Psalm 89, 'My song shall be alway of the loving-kindness of the Lord,' and latterly with Psalm 122, 'I was glad when they said unto me,' while the King goes up to the chair of estate (not, of course, the throne).

The Recognition follows, the Archbishop showing the King to the people, east, south, west, and north, much as at present.

During the succeeding anthem the Archbishop vests at the altar, and then the King makes the first oblations, an altar frontal and a pound of gold, the Archbishop adding a short prayer.

Then comes the Sermon, the King sitting in the chair of estate.

The Oath follows administered after certain questions have been put to the King, the first being:

'Sir, will you grant and keep and by your oath, confirm, to the people of England, the Laws and Customs to them granted by the kings of England, your lawful and religious predecessors; and namely the laws, customs, and franchise granted to the clergy by the glorious King S. Edward, your predecessor according to the laws of God, the true profession of the Gospel established in the church of England, and agreeable to the prerogative of the king thereof, and the ancient customs of this realm?'

The oath is sworn to by the King upon the altar.

The King kneels at his faldstool, while the Archbishop begins the hymn '*Veni, Creator*,' and the quire sings it, the longer form in many verses being used in the English version of the service as in the ordination of priests.

After '*Veni, Creator*,' the Archbishop says a short prayer and then two Bishops or two chanters sing the Litany which includes a special petition for the King.

Three very long prayers follow. The first is quoted as typical of the others. It contains the clause which came down from Saxon times praying that the King may nourish and teach and defend and instruct the Church and people.

'O Almighty God, and everlasting Father, Creator of all good things, King of Kings, Lord of Lords, who didst cause thy faithful servant Abraham, to Triumph over his enemies, didst give many victories to Moses and Joshua the Governors of thy people; didst exalt thy lowly servant David unto the height of a Kingdom; and didst enrich Solomon with the unspeakable gift of Wisdom and Peace: Give ear we beseech thee unto our humble prayers, and multiply thy blessings upon this thy Servant CHARLES, whom in lowly devotion we do consecrate our King that he being strengthened with the faith of Abraham, endued with the mildness of Moses, armed with the fortitude of Joshua, exalted with the humility of David, beautified with the Wisdom of Solomon, he may please thee in all things, he may always walk uprightly in the way of righteousness, he may nourish and teach, and defend and instruct, thy Church and People, and like a mighty King, Minister to them the government of this virtue, against all enemies visible and invisible, and by thy help reform their minds to the concord of thy faith and peace that being under-propped by the due obedience and honoured by the condign love of this his people, he may by thy mercy royal ascend up to the throne of his forefathers; and being defended with the helmet of thy protection, covered with thy invincible shield, and all clad with heavenly armour, he may gloriously triumph, and by his power both terrify infidels, and bring joyful peace to those that fight for thee through our Lord, who by the power of his Cross, hath destroyed hell; and having overthrown the kingdom of the devil, is with the victory ascended into heaven, in whom does consist all power, wisdom, and victory, who is the glory of the humble, the life and salvation of his people, who liveth with thee, and the Holy Ghost, now and for ever. *Amen.*'

After the three long prayers there is the following short one, quoted here because it afterwards became the collect in the Communion Service.

'God which providest for thy people by thy power, and rulest over them in love, grant unto thy Servant CHARLES, the Spirit of Wisdom and Government that being devoted unto thee with all his heart, he may so wisely govern this Kingdom, that in his time the Church may be in safety, and Christian devotion may continue in peace, that persevering to the end in good Works, he may by thy mercy come unto thine everlasting Kingdom, through thy Son our Lord Jesus Christ, who liveth and reigneth with thee and the Holy Ghost, world without end. *Amen*.'

Then follows the proper preface to the act of consecration.

The Litany being ended the Archbishop begins:

'Lift up your hearts.'

Answer. 'We lift them up unto the Lord.'

Archbishop. 'Let us give thanks unto our Lord God.'

Answer. 'It is meet and right so to do.'

Archbishop. 'It is very meet, right, and our bounden duties, that we should at all times, and in all places, give thanks unto thee O Lord, holy Father, Almighty and everlasting God, the strength of thy Chosen, and the exalter of the humble, who in the beginning by the pouring out of thy flood, didst chasten the sin of the World, and by a dove conveying an olive branch, didst give a token of reconcilement unto the earth: And again didst consecrate thy servant Aaron a priest, by the anointing of oil and afterwards by the effusion of oil didst make Kings and Prophets to govern thy people Israel: and by the voice of the Prophet David didst foretell that the countenance of the Church should be made cheerful with oil: We beseech thee, Almighty Father, that by the fatness of thy creature, thou wilt vouchsafe to bless and sanctify thy servant CHARLES, that in the simplicity of a dove he may minister peace unto his people, that he may imitate Aaron in the service of God;

that he may attain the perfection of Government, in counsel and judgment: And that by the anointing of this oil, thou mayest give him a countenance always cheerful and amiable to the whole people, through Jesus Christ our Lord. *Amen.*'

Which being ended, the King arises from his devotions, and after he hath a while reposed himself in his chair of estate, he arises and goes to the altar, and there disrobes himself of his upper garment. His Majesty's under-garments being made so as the places to be anointed may be opened by the undoing of certain loops. The Archbishop undoes those loops and opens the places to be anointed.

The chair on which he is to be anointed being ready the Archbishop first anoints him on the palms of both his hands, saying,

'Let these hands be anointed with holy oil, as Kings and Prophets have been anointed, and as Samuel did anoint David to be King: so that thou may be blessed and established a King in this Kingdom over this people, whom the Lord thy God has given thee to rule and govern, which may he vouchsafe to grant, who with the Father, and Holy Ghost, three in person, and one in unity, be blessed and praised now and for evermore. *Amen.*'

Then the quire sings the anthem 'Zadock the Priest' and the Archbishop says another long prayer, and then proceeds with the anointing.

1. On the Breast.
2. Between the Shoulders.
3. On both the Shoulders.
4. The two boughs of both the Arms.
5. The crown of the Head in manner of a cross.

The anointing being done, the Dean of Westminster closes the loops which were opened.

Then the Archbishop says two more prayers.

A shallow coif is then put upon the King's head, because of the anointing.

Then the Colobium Sindonis, formed like a Dalmatic, is put upon him.

After which the Archbishop says this prayer:

'O God, the King of Kings, by whom Kings do reign, and lawgivers make good Laws, Vouchsafe in thy favour to bless this kingly ornament; and grant that thy Servant CHARLES our King, who shall wear it, may shine in thy sight with the ornament of good life and holy actions, and after this life, he may for ever enjoy that life and glory which has no end; through Jesus Christ our Lord. *Amen.*'

The prayer being done, the Dean of Westminster arrays the King (1) with the Supertunica or Close Pall; (2) with the Tinsin Hose; (3) with the Sandals.

The Spurs are put on by a Nobleman thereunto appointed.

Then the Archbishop takes the King's own sword and lays it on the altar and says:

'Hear our Prayers we beseech thee, O Lord, and vouchsafe by the right hand of thy Majesty to bless and sanctify this Sword wherewith this thy Servant CHARLES desires to be girt; that it may be a defence and protection of churches, widows, orphans, and all the servants of God, against the savage cruelty of pagans and infidels, and that it may be a fear and terror to all those that lay in wait to do mischief; through Jesus Christ our Lord. *Amen.*'

Then the Archbishop and Bishops assisting, deliver the Sword, the Archbishop saying:

'Receive the sword by the hands of the Bishops.'

The Sword is girt about him by a Peer, thereunto appointed, the Archbishop saying:

'Receive this Kingly sword, which is hallowed for the defence of the holy Church; and delivered unto thee by the hands of bishops though unworthy, yet consecrated by the authority of the holy Apostles: and remember those of whom the Psalmist did prophesy saying, Gird thee with thy sword upon thy thigh (O thou most mighty) and with this sword exercise the force of equity, and mightily destroy the growth of iniquity, protect the holy Church of God, and his faithful people, and pursue hereticks no less than infidels; defend and help widows and orphans, restore the things that are gone to decay, maintain the things that are restored. Be avenged of injustice and confirm the things that are in good order, that doing these things thou may be glorious in triumph of virtue and excellent in the ornament of justice, and reign for ever with the Saviour of the World, whom in name thou dost represent, Christ our Lord, to whom with the Father and the Holy Ghost, be power and dominion now and for ever. *Amen*.'

Then is the Armill put about his neck, and tied to the boughs of his arms, the Archbishop saying:

'Receive the Bracelets of sincerity and wisdom, as a token of God's embracing whereby all thy works may be defended against thy enemies both bodily and ghostly, through Christ our Lord. *Amen*.'

Then is the Mantle or open Pall put upon him by the Dean of Westminster, the Archbishop saying:

THE IMPERIAL STATE CROWN
Put on after the service

THE ROYAL SCEPTRE
Held in the Queen's right hand

'Receive this Pall which is formed with four corners to let thee understand that the four corners of the World are subject to the power of God: and that no man can happily reign upon earth, who has not received his authority from heaven. *Amen.*'

Then the Archbishop takes the Crown into his hands, and lays it before him upon the altar, and says this prayer:

'God the Crown of the faithful, who crowned their heads with a crown of precious Stone that trust in thee; Bless and sanctify this Crown, that as the same is adorned with divers precious stones, so this thy servant that weareth it, may be filled with thy manifold graces, and all precious virtues, through the King eternal thy Son our Lord. *Amen.*'

Then the Archbishop crowns the King, saying:

'God Crown thee with a crown of glory and righteousness, with the honour and work of fortitude, that thou by our Ministry, having a right faith, and manifold fruit of good works, may obtain the crown of an everlasting Kingdom, by the gift of him whose Kingdom endures for ever. *Amen.*'

Then the Archbishop says two prayers of blessing, and in the meantime the quire sings the anthem '*Confortare,*' etc., and Psalm 21, '*Domine, in virtute.*'

Then the Archbishop takes the King's ring and says this prayer:

'Bless, O Lord, and sanctify this Ring, that thy servant wearing it, may be sealed with the ring of faith, and by the power of the highest, be preserved from sin. And let the blessings that are found in holy scriptures, plentifully descend upon him, that whatsoever he shall sanctify may be holy, and whatsoever he shall bless may be blessed. *Amen.*'

Then he puts the Ring on the fourth finger of the King's right hand, saying:

'Receive the Ring of kingly dignity, and be it the seal of Christian Catholic faith, that as this day thou art adorned the head and prince of this Kingdom and People, so thou may persevere as the protector and establisher of Christianity, and the Christian Faith, that being rich in faith, and happy in works, thou may reign with him that is King of Kings, to whom be honour and glory for ever and ever. *Amen.*'

After the Ring is put on, the Archbishop says this prayer:

'O God, to whom belongeth all power and dignity, give unto thy servant CHARLES the fruit of his dignity, wherein grant he may long continue, and fear thee always; and always labour to please thee, through Christ our Lord. *Amen.*'

Then the King puts on the Gloves, part of the Regalia, because of the anointing.

Then he takes his sword, with which he was girt before; with it he goes to the altar, and there offers it up.

The chief Peer then present, redeems the Sword, takes it from the altar, draws it out, and so carries it before the King, from that time, during the whole solemnity.

Then the Archbishop takes the sceptre with the cross, and delivers it into the King's right hand, saying:

'Receive the sceptre, the sign of kingly power, the rod of the Kingdom, the rod of virtue, that thou may govern thyself aright, and defend the holy Church, and Christian people, committed by God unto thy charge: punish the wicked, and protect the just: and lead them in the way of righteousness, that from this temporal

Kingdom thou may be advanced to an eternal Kingdom, by his goodness, whose Kingdom is everlasting. *Amen.*'

Then the Archbishop says this prayer:

'O Lord, the fountain of all good things, and the author of all good proceedings: grant, we beseech thee, to this thy servant CHARLES that he may order aright the dignity which he has obtained. Vouchsafe to confirm the honour that thou have given him: Honour him before all kings: establish him in the throne of this Realm: visit him with the increase of Children: let Justice spring up in his days: and with joy and gladness let him reign in thy everlasting Kingdom. *Amen.*'

Then the Archbishop delivers the Rod with the Dove into the King's left hand, saying:

'Receive the Rod of virtue and equity, learn to make much of the godly, to terrify the wicked: shew the way to those that go astray: repress the proud: lift up the lowly: that our Lord Jesus Christ may open to thee the door, who says of himself, I am the Door, by me if any man enter, he shall be safe: And let him be thy helper, who is the Key of David, and the Sceptre of the house of Israel, who opens and no man shuts, who shuts and no man opens, who brings the captive out of prison, where he sat in darkness and in the shadow of death: that in all things thou may follow him, of whom the prophet David said, The sceptre of thy kingdom is a right sceptre, thou hast loved righteousness, and hated iniquity: where-fore God, even thy God, has anointed thee with the oil of gladness above thy fellows; even Jesus Christ our Lord. *Amen.*'

After this he blesses the King, saying:

'The Lord bless thee, and keep thee, and as he has made thee King over his people; so he still prosper thee in this

World and make thee partaker of his eternal felicity in the World to come. *Amen.*'

The King being thus crowned and invested he vouchsafes to kiss the Archbishop and the Bishops that were assisting at his coronation.

This done, the King goes from the altar to his stage, the throne royal.

All the Bishops and other Peers every one in his place attending him, the Archbishop will say:

'Grant, O Lord, that the Clergy and People gathered together by this ordinance for this service of the King, may by the most gracious assistance of thy goodness, and the vigilant care of thy Servant the King, be continually governed and preserved in all happiness. *Amen.*'

Then the quire sings '*Te Deum Laudamus.*' Afterwards the King is lifted up into his throne by the Archbishop and Bishops, and being enthroned or placed therein, the Archbishop says:

'Stand and hold fast from henceforth the place whereof hitherto thou hast been heir, by the succession of thy forefathers, being now delivered unto thee by the authority of Almighty God, and by the hands of us, and all the Bishops and servants of God. And as thou see the Clergy to come nearer to the altar so remember that in places convenient you give them greater honour, that the Mediator of God and Man, may establish you in this Kingly throne, to be the mediator between the Clergy and the laity; and that thou may reign for ever with Jesus Christ, the King of Kings, and the Lord of Lords; who with the Father and the Holy Ghost, liveth and reigneth for ever. *Amen.*'

Fealty and homage are then done by the Bishops and Peers much as at present.

The Coronation Service itself having been completed, the Mass followed in the Latin service, the Prayer Book rite being used when the service was translated into English. The Epistle and Gospel were the same in both rites.

At the offertory, as in the modern service, the King descends from his throne and offers the sacred elements.

The Archbishop then says:

'Bless, O Lord, we beseech thee, these thy gifts and sanctify them unto this holy use, that by them we may be made partakers of the Body and Blood of thine only-begotten son Jesus Christ, and thy servant CHARLES may be fed unto everlasting life, in soul and body, and enabled to discharge this great office, whereunto thou hast called him of thy great goodness. Grant this, O Lord, for the honour of Jesus Christ his sake, our only mediator and advocate. *Amen.*'

And then the King returns back to his chair, and after a while he comes the second time to the altar, and there offers *Vnam Marcam Auri*.

He kneels down and the Archbishop says two long blessings.

The King kneeling still at the steps of the altar, the Archbishop proceeds to the consecration of the Sacrament: and having communicated himself

He administers the body
And the Dean of Westminster the cup } to the King.

When the Communion is ended, the King returns to his throne.

In the meantime the quire sings the anthem, 'O hearken thou,' etc.

After the anthem, the Archbishop reads the last prayers; and the quire sings, 'Glory be to God,' etc.

And so the Communion ends.

Then the King, accompanied and attended as before, goes into S. Edward's Chapel from his throne, in state.

And at the altar the Archbishop takes off the King's crown and lays it upon the altar there.

The King withdraws himself into the Traverse prepared for him.

In the Traverse the Great Chamberlain of England disrobes the King of S. Edward's Robes, and forthwith delivers them to the Dean of Westminster, who brings them, and lays them upon the altar.

Then is the King newly arrayed with the Robes prepared for his Majesty wearing that day, and laid ready in the Traverse, to the end that by the Great Chamberlain they may be put on.

The King being thus newly arrayed, comes from the Traverse to S. Edward's altar.

The Archbishop, invested still in the same manner he was at the Communion, sets the Crown Imperial (provided for the King to wear that day) upon his head.

The King so crowned taking into his hands each of them, the Sceptre and the Rod (after the Train is set in order before them), goes from S. Edward's Altar up to the stage; and so through the midst of the quire and church out of the west door, and returns to the Palace the same way he came, with great glory.

The Sceptre and Rod of S. Edward which the King carries in his hands are, after Dinner (when the King withdraws himself into his chamber), to be delivered to the Church of Westminster to be kept as heretofore they have been, with the residue of the *Regalia*.

THE FORM AND ORDER

OBSERVED IN

THE CORONATION OF HIS MAJESTY KING GEORGE VI

IN THE

ABBEY CHURCH OF S. PETER

WESTMINSTER

ON WEDNESDAY THE 12TH

DAY OF MAY

1937

ADAPTED[1]

[1] In this reprint all that pertains to the Queen Consort is omitted.

THE FORM AND ORDER

OF

HIS MAJESTY'S CORONATION

I

THE PREPARATION

In the morning upon the day of the Coronation early, care is to be taken that the Ampulla be filled with Oil and, together with the Spoon, be laid ready upon the Altar in the Abbey Church.

The Litany shall be sung as the Dean and Prebendaries and the Choir of Westminster proceed from the Altar to the West door of the Church.

The Archbishops and Bishops Assistant being already vested in their Copes, the procession shall be formed immediately outside of the West door of the Church, and shall wait till notice is given of the approach of his Majesty, and shall then begin to move into the Church.

II

THE ENTRANCE INTO THE CHURCH

The King, as soon as he enters at the West door of the Church, is to be received with the following Anthem, to be sung by the choir of Westminster.

Psalm cxxii. 1–3, 6, 7

I was glad when they said unto me, We will go into the house of the Lord. Our feet shall stand in thy gates, O Jerusalem. Jerusalem is built as a city that is at unity

THE RECOGNITION
Coronation of George VI

in itself. O pray for the peace of Jerusalem: they shall prosper that love thee. Peace be within thy walls, and plenteousness within thy palaces.

The King shall in the mean time pass up the body of the Church, into and through the Choir, and so up the stairs to the Theatre; and having passed by his throne, he shall make his humble adoration, and then kneeling at the faldstool set for him before his Chair of Estate on the South side of the Altar, use some short private prayers; and after, sit down in his chair.

III

THE RECOGNITION

The King being so placed, the Archbishop, together with the Lord Chancellor, Lord Great Chamberlain, Lord High Constable, and Earl Marshal (Garter King of Arms preceding them), shall go to the East side of the Theatre, and after, shall go to the other three sides in this order, South, West, and North, and at every of the four sides the Archbishop shall with a loud voice speak to the People: and the King in the mean while, standing up by his chair, shall turn and shew himself unto the People at every of the four sides of the Theatre as the Archbishop is at every of them, the Archbishop saying:

SIRS, I here present unto you King GEORGE, your undoubted King: Wherefore all you who are come this day to do your homage and service, Are you willing to do the same?

The People signify their willingness and joy, by loud and repeated acclamations, all with one voice crying out,

God save King George.

Then the trumpets shall sound.

E

The Bible, Paten, and Chalice shall be brought by the Bishops who had borne them, and placed upon the Altar.

The Lords who carry in procession the Regalia, except those who carry the Swords, shall come near to the Altar, and present in order every one what he carries to the Archbishop, who shall deliver them to the Dean of Westminster, to be by him placed upon the Altar.

IV

THE OATH

Then shall the Archbishop go to the King, and standing before him, administer the Coronation Oath, first asking the King,

SIR, is your Majesty willing to take the Oath?

And the King answering,

I am willing,

The Archbishop shall minister these questions; and the King, having a book in his hands, shall answer each question severally as follows:

Archbishop. Will you solemnly promise and swear to govern the peoples of *Great Britain, Ireland, Canada, Australia, New Zealand,* and the Union of *South Africa,* of your Possessions and the other Territories to any of them belonging or pertaining, and of your Empire of *India,* according to their respective laws and customs?

King. I solemnly promise so to do.

Archbishop. Will you to your power cause Law and Justice, in Mercy, to be executed in all your judgements?

King. I will.

Archbishop. Will you to the utmost of your power maintain the Laws of God and the true profession of the

Gospel? Will you to the utmost of your power maintain in the *United Kingdom* the Protestant Reformed Religion established by law? And will you maintain and preserve inviolably the settlement of the Church of *England*, and the doctrine, worship, discipline, and government thereof, as by law established in *England*? And will you preserve unto the Bishops and Clergy of *England*, and to the Churches there committed to their charge, all such rights and privileges, as by law do or shall appertain to them, or any of them?

King. All this I promise to do.

Then the King arising out of his chair, supported as before, and assisted by the Lord Great Chamberlain, the Sword of State being carried before him, shall go to the Altar, and there being uncovered, make his solemn Oath in the sight The Bible to *of all the people, to observe the premisses: laying his* be brought: *right hand upon the Holy Gospel in the Great Bible* (*which was before carried in the Procession and is now brought from the Altar by the Archbishop, and tendered to him as he kneels upon the steps*), *saying these words:*

THE things which I have here before promised, I will perform, and keep. So help me God.

Then the King shall kiss the Book and sign the And a silver *Oath.* Standish

The King having thus taken his Oath shall return again to his chair, and the Archbishop shall go to him and minister the Declaration prescribed by Act of Parliament, and his Majesty shall make, subscribe, and audibly repeat the same. This done, the Archbishop shall return to the Altar and begin the Communion Service.

V

THE BEGINNING OF THE COMMUNION SERVICE

THE INTROIT

LET my prayer come up into thy presence as the incense: and let the lifting up of my hands be as an evening sacrifice.

Then the Archbishop shall begin the Communion Service, saying:

The Lord be with you.

Answer. And with thy spirit.

Let us pray

O GOD, who providest for thy people by thy power, and rulest over them in love: Grant unto this thy servant GEORGE, our King, the Spirit of wisdom and government, that being devoted unto thee with all his heart, he may so wisely govern, that in his time thy Church and people may continue in safety and prosperity; and that, persevering in good works unto the end, he may through thy mercy come to thine everlasting kingdom; through Jesus Christ our Lord, who liveth and reigneth with thee and the Holy Ghost, ever one God, world without end. *Amen.*

THE EPISTLE

To be read by one of the Bishops

1 S. Peter ii. 13

SUBMIT yourselves to every ordinance of man for the Lord's sake: . . . Honour the king.

THE GOSPEL

To be read by another Bishop, the King with the people standing

S. Matthew xxii. 15

THEN went the Pharisees, . . . went their way.

Then shall be sung the Creed following, the King with the people standing, as before

I BELIEVE in one God . . . world to come. Amen.

VI

THE ANOINTING

The Creed being ended, the King kneeling at his faldstool, the Archbishop shall begin the hymn, VENI, CREATOR SPIRITUS, *and the choir shall sing it out.*

COME, Holy Ghost, our souls inspire, . . .

This being ended, the Archbishop shall say this prayer:

O LORD, Holy Father, who by anointing with Oil didst of old make and consecrate kings, priests, and prophets, to teach and govern thy people Israel: Bless and sanctify thy chosen servant GEORGE, who by our office and ministry is now to be anointed with this Oil [*here the Archbishop is to lay his hand upon the Ampulla*], and consecrated King: Strengthen him, O Lord, with the Holy Ghost the Comforter; confirm and stablish him with thy free and princely Spirit, the Spirit of wisdom and government, the Spirit of counsel and ghostly strength, the Spirit of knowledge and true godliness, and fill him, O Lord, with the Spirit of thy holy fear, now and for ever. *Amen.*

This prayer being ended, the choir shall sing:

1 Kings i. 39, 40

ZADOK the priest and Nathan the prophet anointed Solomon king; and all the people rejoiced and said: God save the king, Long live the king, May the king live for ever. Amen. Hallelujah.

In the mean time, the King rising from his devotions, having been disrobed of his crimson robe by the Lord Great Chamberlain, and having taken off his cap of state, shall go before the Altar, supported and attended as before.

The King shall sit down in King Edward's Chair (placed in the midst of the area over against the Altar, with a faldstool before it), wherein he is to be anointed. Four Knights of the Garter shall hold over him a rich pall of silk, or cloth of gold: The Dean of Westminster, taking the Ampulla and Spoon from off the Altar, shall hold them ready, pouring some of the holy Oil into the Spoon, and with it the Archbishop shall anoint the King in the form of a cross:

I. *On the palms of both the hands, saying,*

Be thy Hands anointed with holy Oil.

II. *On the breast, saying,*

Be thy Breast anointed with holy Oil.

III. *On the crown of the head, saying,*

BE thy Head anointed with holy Oil, as kings, priests, and prophets were anointed: And as Solomon was anointed king by Zadok the priest and Nathan the prophet, so be you anointed, blessed, and consecrated King over the Peoples, whom the Lord your God hath given you to rule and govern, In the Name of the Father, and of the Son, and of the Holy Ghost. Amen.

Then shall the Dean of Westminster lay the Ampulla and Spoon upon the Altar; and the King kneeling down at the fald-stool, the Archbishop standing shall say this Blessing over him:

OUR Lord Jesus Christ, the Son of God, who by his Father was anointed with the Oil of gladness above his fellows, by his holy Anointing pour down upon your Head and Heart the blessing of the Holy Ghost, and prosper the works of your Hands: that by the assistance of his heavenly grace you may preserve the people committed to your charge in wealth, peace, and godli-ness; and after a long and glorious course of ruling a temporal kingdom wisely, justly, and religiously, you may at last be made partaker of an eternal kingdom, through Jesus Christ our Lord. *Amen.*

This prayer being ended, the King shall arise and sit down again in King Edward's Chair, while the Knights of the Garter give back the pall to the Lord Chamberlain; whereupon the King again arising, the Dean of Westminster shall put upon his Majesty the Colobium Sindonis and the Supertunica or close pall of cloth of gold, together with a Girdle of the same. Then shall the King again sit down.

VII

THE PRESENTING OF THE SPURS AND SWORD, AND THE GIRDING AND OBLATION OF THE SAID SWORD

The Spurs shall be brought from the Altar by the Dean of Westminster, and delivered to the Lord Great Chamberlain; who, kneeling down, shall touch his Majesty's heels therewith, and send them back to the Altar.

Then the Lord, who carries the Sword of State, delivering to the Lord Chamberlain the said Sword (which is thereupon deposited in the traverse in Saint Edward's Chapel) shall receive from the Lord Chamberlain, in lieu thereof, another Sword in a scabbard of purple velvet, provided for the King to be girt withal, which he shall deliver to the Archbishop; and the Archbishop shall lay it on the Altar, saying the following prayer:

HEAR our prayers, O Lord, we beseech thee, and so direct and support thy servant King GEORGE, who is now to be girt with this Sword, that he may not bear it in vain; but may use it as the minister of God for the terror and punishment of evildoers, and for the protection and encouragement of those that do well, through Jesus Christ our Lord. *Amen.*

Then shall the Archbishop take the Sword from off the Altar, and deliver it into the King's right hand, the Archbishop of York and the Bishops of London and Winchester and other Bishops assisting and going along with him; and, the King holding it, the Archbishop shall say:

RECEIVE this kingly Sword, brought now from the Altar of God, and delivered to you by the hands of us the Bishops and servants of God, though unworthy.

The King standing up, the Sword shall be girt about him by the Lord Great Chamberlain; and then, the King sitting down, the Archbishop shall say:

WITH this Sword do justice, stop the growth of iniquity, protect the holy Church of God, help and defend widows and orphans, restore the things that are gone to decay, maintain the things that are restored, punish and reform what is amiss, and confirm what is in good order: that doing these things you may be glorious in all virtue;

and so faithfully serve our Lord Jesus Christ in this life, that you may reign for ever with him in the life which is to come.

Then the King, rising up, shall ungird his Sword, and, going to the Altar, offer it there in the scabbard, and then return and sit down in King Edward's Chair: and the Peer, who first received the Sword, shall offer the price of it, namely, one hundred shillings, and having thus redeemed it, shall receive it from the Dean of Westminster, from off the Altar, and draw it out of the scabbard, and carry it naked before his Majesty during the rest of the solemnity.
Then the Bishops who have assisted during the offering shall return to their places.

VIII

THE INVESTING WITH THE ARMILL AND ROYAL ROBE, AND THE DELIVERY OF THE ORB

Then the King arising, the Armill and Robe Royal or Pall of cloth of gold shall be delivered by the Officer of the Great Wardrobe to the Dean of Westminster, and by him put upon the King, standing; the Lord Great Chamberlain fastening the clasps. Then shall the King sit down, and the Orb with the Cross shall be brought from the Altar by the Dean of Westminster, and delivered into the King's hand by the Archbishop, pronouncing this Blessing and exhortation:

RECEIVE this Imperial Robe, and Orb; and the Lord your God endue you with knowledge and wisdom, with majesty and with power from on high; the Lord embrace you with his mercy on every side; the Lord clothe you with the robe of righteousness, and with the garments of salvation. And when you see this Orb thus set under the Cross, remember that the whole world is subject to the Power and Empire of Christ our Redeemer.

Then shall the King deliver his Orb to the Dean of Westminster, to be by him laid on the Altar.

IX

THE INVESTITURE *PER ANNULUM ET BACULUM*

Then the Keeper of the Jewel House shall deliver to the Archbishop the King's Ring, in which a table jewel is enchased: the Archbishop shall put it on the fourth finger of his Majesty's right hand, and say:

RECEIVE this Ring, the ensign of kingly dignity, and of defence of the Catholic Faith; and as you are this day solemnly invested in the government of an earthly kingdom, so may you be sealed with that Spirit of promise, which is the earnest of an heavenly inheritance, and reign with him who is the blessed and only Potentate, to whom be glory for ever and ever. Amen.

Then shall the Dean of Westminster bring the Sceptre with the Cross and the Sceptre with the Dove to the Archbishop.
The Gloves, presented by the Lord of the Manor of Worksop, being put on, the Archbishop shall deliver the Sceptre with the Cross into the King's right hand, saying,

RECEIVE the Royal Sceptre, the ensign of kingly power and justice.

And then shall he deliver the Sceptre with the Dove into the King's left hand, and say:

RECEIVE the Rod of equity and mercy: and God, from whom all holy desires, all good counsels, and all just works do proceed, direct, and assist you in the administration and exercise of all those powers which he hath given you. Be so merciful that you be not too remiss; so execute justice that you forget not mercy. Punish the wicked, protect and cherish the just, and lead your people in the way wherein they should go.

The Lord of the Manor of Worksop may support his Majesty's right arm.

X

THE PUTTING ON OF THE CROWN

The Archbishop, standing before the Altar, shall take the Crown into his hands, and laying it again before him upon the Altar, he shall say: S. Edward's Crown

O GOD, the crown of the faithful: Bless we beseech thee and sanctify this thy servant GEORGE our King: and as thou dost this day set a Crown of pure *Here the King* gold upon his head, so enrich his royal heart *must be put in mind to bow* with thine abundant grace, and crown him *his head* with all princely virtues, through the King eternal Jesus Christ our Lord. *Amen.*

Then the King still sitting in King Edward's Chair, the Archbishop, assisted with other Bishops, shall come from the Altar: the Dean of Westminster shall bring the Crown, and the Archbishop taking it of him shall reverently put it upon the King's head. At the sight whereof the people, with loud and repeated shouts, shall cry,

𝕲𝖔𝖉 𝖘𝖆𝖛𝖊 𝖙𝖍𝖊 𝕶𝖎𝖓𝖌;

the Peers and the Kings of Arms shall put on their coronets; and the trumpets shall sound, and by a signal given, the great guns at the Tower shall be shot off.

The acclamation ceasing, the Archbishop shall go on, and say:

GOD crown you with a crown of glory and righteousness, that by the ministry of this our benediction,
having a right faith and manifold fruit of good works,
you may obtain the crown of an everlasting kingdom
by the gift of him whose kingdom endureth for ever.
Amen.

Then shall the choir sing:

BE strong and play the man: keep the commandments
of the Lord thy God, and walk in his ways.

XI

THE PRESENTING OF THE HOLY BIBLE

*Then shall the Dean of Westminster take the Holy Bible
from off the Altar, and deliver it to the Archbishop, who shall
present it to the King, first saying these words to him:*

OUR gracious King; we present you with this Book,
the most valuable thing that this world affords. Here is
wisdom; this is the royal Law; these are the lively
Oracles of God.

*Then shall the King deliver back the Bible to the Archbishop,
who shall give it to the Dean of Westminster, to be reverently
placed again upon the holy Altar; and the Archbishop of York
and the Bishops shall return to their places.*

XII

THE BENEDICTION

*And now the King having been thus anointed and crowned,
and having received all the ensigns of royalty, the Archbishop
shall solemnly bless him: and the Archbishop of York and all*

the Bishops, with the rest of the Peers, shall follow every part
of the Benediction with a loud and hearty Amen.

THE Lord bless you and keep you: and as he hath made
you King over his people, so may he prosper you in
this world, and make you partake of his eternal felicity
in the world to come. *Amen.*

THE Lord give you fruitful lands and healthful seasons;
victorious fleets and armies, and a quiet Empire; a faithful Senate, wise and upright counsellors and magistrates,
a loyal nobility, and a dutiful gentry; a pious and learned
and useful clergy; an honest, peaceable, and obedient
commonalty. *Amen.*

Then shall the Archbishop turn to the people, and say:

AND the same Lord God Almighty grant, that the
Clergy and Nobles assembled here for this great and
solemn service, and together with them all the people
of the land, fearing God, and honouring the King, may
by the merciful superintendency of the divine Providence,
and the vigilant care of our gracious Sovereign, continually enjoy peace, plenty, and prosperity; through Jesus
Christ our Lord, to whom, with the eternal Father, and
God the Holy Ghost, be glory in the Church, world
without end. *Amen.*

XIII

THE INTHRONIZATION

Then shall the King go to his Throne, and be lifted up into it
by the Archbishops and Bishops, and other Peers of the
Kingdom; and being Inthronized, or placed therein, all the Great
Officers, those that bear the Swords and the Sceptres, and the
Nobles who carried the other Regalia, shall stand round about

the steps of the Throne; and the Archbishop standing before the King, shall say:

STAND firm, and hold fast from henceforth the seat and state of royal and imperial dignity, which is this day delivered unto you, in the Name and by the authority of Almighty God, and by the hands of us the Bishops and servants of God, though unworthy: And as you see us to approach nearer to God's Altar, so vouchsafe the more graciously to continue to us your royal favour and protection. And the Lord God Almighty, whose ministers we are, and the stewards of his mysteries, establish your Throne in righteousness, that it may stand fast for evermore, like as the sun before him, and as the faithful witness in heaven. *Amen.*

XIV

THE HOMAGE

The Exhortation being ended, all the Princes and Peers then present shall do their Homage publicly and solemnly unto the King.

The Archbishop first shall kneel down before his Majesty's knees, and the rest of the Bishops shall kneel in their places: and they shall do their Homage together, for the shortening of the ceremony, the Archbishop saying:

I . . . . Archbishop of *Canterbury* [*and so every one of the rest,* I N. Bishop of N., *repeating the rest audibly after the Archbishop*] will be faithful and true, and faith and truth will bear unto you our Sovereign Lord, and your heirs Kings of *Great Britain, Ireland,* and the British Dominions beyond the Seas, Defenders of the Faith, and Emperors of India. And I will do, and truly acknowledge, the service of the lands which I claim to hold of you, as in right of the Church. So help me God.

Then shall the Archbishop kiss the King's left cheek.
Then the Duke of Gloucester, taking off his Coronet, shall kneel down before his Majesty's knees, the rest of the Princes of the Blood Royal, being Peers of the Realm, kneeling in their places, taking off their Coronets, and pronouncing the words of Homage after him, the Duke of Gloucester saying:

I N. Prince, or Duke, &c., of N. do become your liege man of life and limb, and of earthly worship; and faith and truth I will bear unto you, to live and die, against all manner of folks. So help me God.

Then shall the Princes of the Blood Royal, being Peers of the Realm, arising severally touch the Crown on his Majesty's head and kiss his Majesty's left cheek. After which the other Peers of the Realm, who are then in their seats, shall kneel down, put off their Coronets, and do their Homage, the Dukes first by themselves, and so the Marquesses, the Earls, the Viscounts, and the Barons, severally in their places, the first of each Order kneeling before his Majesty, and the others of his Order who are near his Majesty also kneeling in their places, and all of his Order saying after him:

I N. Duke, or Earl, &c., of N. do become your liege man of life and limb, and of earthly worship; and faith and truth I will bear unto you, to live and die, against all manner of folks. So help me God.

The Peers having done their Homage, the first of each Order, putting off his Coronet, shall singly ascend the throne, and stretching forth his hand, touch the Crown on his Majesty's head, as promising by that ceremony for himself and his Order to be ever ready to support it with all their power; and then shall he kiss the King's cheek.

While the Princes and Peers are thus doing their Homage, the King, if he thinks good, shall deliver his Sceptre with the Cross and the Sceptre or Rod with the Dove, to some one near to the Blood Royal, or to the Lords that carried them in the procession, or to any other that he pleaseth to assign, to hold them by him. And the Bishops that support the King in the procession may also ease him, by supporting the Crown, as there shall be occasion. At the same time the choir shall sing these anthems:

O COME ye servants of the Lord, and praise his holy name.

From early morn to setting sun, his might on earth proclaim.

His laws are just, and glad the heart; he makes his mercies known:

Ye princes come, ye people too, and bow before his throne.

CHRISTOPHER TYE

HEAR my prayer, O Lord, and let my crying come unto Thee.

HENRY PURCELL

O CLAP your hands together, all ye people, O sing unto God with the voice of melody. For the Lord is high, and to be feared: He is the great King of all the earth. He shall subdue the people under us, and the nations under our feet. He shall choose out an heritage for us, even the worship of Jacob, whom he loved.

ORLANDO GIBBONS

ALL the ends of the world shall remember themselves, and be turned unto the Lord: and all the kindreds of the nations shall worship before Him.　　WILLIAM BOYCE

O PRAISE GOD in his holiness : praise him in the firmament of his power.

Praise him in his noble acts : praise him according to his excellent greatness.

THE HOMAGE OF THE PEERS
Coronation of George VI

Praise him in the sound of the trumpet : praise him upon the lute and harp.

Praise him in the cymbals and dances : praise him upon the strings and pipe.

Praise him upon the well-tuned cymbals : praise him upon the loud cymbals.

Let everything that hath breath praise the Lord.

GEORGE DYSON

Thou wilt keep him in perfect peace, whose mind is stayed on Thee. The darkness is no darkness with Thee, but the night is as clear as the day: the darkness and the light to Thee are both alike. God is light, and in Him is no darkness at all. O let my soul live, and it shall praise Thee. For Thine is the Kingdom, the power, and the glory for evermore.

Thou wilt keep him in perfect peace, whose mind is stayed on Thee. SAMUEL SEBASTIAN WESLEY

When the Homage is ended, the drums shall beat, and the trumpets sound, and all the people shout, crying out:

God save King George.

Long live King George.

May the King live for ever.

The solemnity of the King's Coronation being thus ended, the Archbishop shall leave the King in his throne and go to the Altar.

F

XV

THE COMMUNION

Then shall the organ play and the choir sing the Offertory.

O HEARKEN thou unto the voice of my calling, my King and my God: for unto thee will I make my prayer.

In the mean while the King shall deliver his Sceptres to the Lords who had previously borne them, and descend from his throne, supported and attended as before; and go to the steps of the Altar, where, taking off his Crown, which he shall deliver to the Lord Great Chamberlain and other appointed Officer to hold, he shall kneel down.

And first the King shall offer Bread and Wine for the Communion, which being brought out of Saint Edward's Chapel, and delivered into his hands (the Bread upon the Paten by the Bishop that read the Epistle, and the Wine in the Chalice by the Bishop that read the Gospel), shall by the Archbishop be received from the King, and reverently placed upon the Altar, and decently covered with a fair linen cloth, the Archbishop first saying this prayer:

BLESS, O Lord, we beseech thee, these thy gifts, and sanctify them unto this holy use, that by them we may be made partakers of the Body and Blood of thine only-begotten Son Jesus Christ, and fed unto everlasting life of soul and body: And that thy servant King GEORGE may be enabled to the discharge of his weighty office, whereunto of thy great goodness thou hast called and appointed him. Grant this, O Lord, for Jesus Christ's sake, our only Mediator and Advocate. *Amen.*

Then the King kneeling, as before, shall make his Oblation, offering a Pall or Altar-cloth delivered by the Officer of the

Great Wardrobe to the Lord Great Chamberlain, and by him, kneeling, to his Majesty, and an Ingot or Wedge of Gold of a pound weight, which the Treasurer of the Household shall deliver to the Lord Great Chamberlain, and he to his Majesty; And the Archbishop coming to him, shall receive and place them upon the Altar.

Then shall the King return to his chair, and kneel down at his faldstool, and the Archbishop shall say:

LET us pray for the whole state of Christ's Church . . .

When the Archbishops, and Dean of Westminster, with the Bishops Assistants (namely, those who have read the Epistle and the Gospel), have communicated in both kinds, the King shall advance to the steps of the Altar and kneel down, and the Archbishop shall administer the Bread, and the Dean of Westminster the Cup, to him.

At the delivery of the Bread shall be said:

THE Body of our Lord Jesus Christ, which was given for thee, preserve thy body and soul unto everlasting life. Take and eat this in remembrance that Christ died for thee, and feed on him in thy heart by faith with thanksgiving.

At the delivery of the Cup:

THE Blood of our Lord Jesus Christ, which was shed for thee, preserve thy body and soul unto everlasting life. Drink this in remembrance that Christ's Blood was shed for thee, and be thankful.

The King shall then put on his Crown, and repair to his Throne, there taking the Sceptre in his hand again.

Then shall the Archbishop go on to the Post-Communion, he and all the people saying,

OUR FATHER, . . .

XVI

Then shall the choir sing:

TE DEUM LAUDAMUS

XVII

THE RECESS

In the mean time, the King attended and accompanied as before, the four Swords being carried before him, shall descend from his throne crowned, and, carrying his Sceptre and Rod in his hands, go into the area eastward of the Theatre, and pass on through the door on the South side of the Altar into Saint Edward's Chapel; and as they pass by the Altar, the rest of the Regalia, lying upon it, are to be delivered by the Dean of Westminster to the Lords that carried them in the procession, and so they shall proceed in state into the Chapel.

The King being come into the Chapel, the King, standing before the Altar, shall deliver the Sceptre with the Dove to the Archbishop, who shall lay it upon the Altar there. And the golden Spurs and Saint Edward's Staff are to be given into the hands of the Dean of Westminster, and by him laid there also.

The King shall then be disrobed of his Royal Robe of State, and arrayed in his Robe of purple velvet, and wearing his Imperial Crown shall then receive in his left hand the Orb from the Archbishop.

Then his Majesty shall proceed through the Choir to the West door of the Church, in the same way as he came, wearing his Crown: the King bearing in his right hand the Sceptre with the Cross, and in his left the Orb; all Peers wearing their Coronets.

FINIS

THE REGALIA

THE ancient regalia were destroyed by the Puritan extremists during the Great Rebellion. Nothing save the spoon for the anointing dates from before the time of Charles II, for whose coronation in 1661 new regalia had to be made. The principal ornaments in the regalia are the Crown of S. Edward (supposed to be a copy of the old one) used for the actual crowning in the service, the Imperial State Crown used subsequently, the five swords, namely, the three carried before the King in the procession, the Sword of Justice to the spirituality on the right, that of Justice to the temporality on the left, the Sword of Mercy with the blunt point, called Curtana, in the middle, beside the sword of State and the King's personal sword. There are the two sceptres, that with the cross (of which the orb is a shortened and altered version) and that with the dove on the top, sometimes called the rod. The spoon is believed to be of the twelfth century and is the only survival of the old regalia, and the ampulla, which is the oil cruet, shaped like an eagle, is said to contain some of the metal of the original.

The Scottish regalia are older. The crown dates from about 1540, and is said to have been reconstructed by French workmen, while the sword was conferred on James IV by Pope Julius II. The last time they were used was for the coronation of Charles II at Scone in 1651. Then for a time they were hidden, first in

Dunnottar Castle, on a great rock almost surrounded by sea, about two miles south of Stonehaven, and then in the parish church of Kinneff not far off.

Taken to Edinburgh, it was stipulated at the Union of the Kingdoms in 1707 that they must remain in Scotland and they were locked up and almost forgotten until George IV, when Prince Regent, ordered them to be brought out and shown to the public in 1818.

THE STONE

IT may be well to give the main facts about the so-called 'Stone of Destiny' taken from Scotland by Edward I in 1296. When brought to Westminster, it was set in the chair in which it is now. This was specially made to hold it, and is a costly and elaborately decorated piece of woodwork. After the recognition of Scottish independence in 1328 we have an original letter from King Edward III to the Abbot of Westminster ordering him to deliver it up to go back to Scotland.[1] But this was never done, and the stone has remained at Westminster ever since.

When James VI of Scotland was crowned upon it in 1603 he appears to have accepted the situation. It has been suggested that this was probably due to the legend that wherever the stone went, Scottish sovereignty would follow it.

The stone has never been brought into the English service in any way and no allusion has been made to it. Actually it belongs to a very different tradition, and is a relic of an early type of ceremony for the inauguration of a chief.

Stripped of legendary accretions, mostly of the wildest kind, it is an example of a primitive inauguration stone which survived from among other such stones and was kept at an ancient religious house at Scone, near Perth. This later on became a house of Augustinian canons.

---

[1] See *English Coronation Records*, Legg, p. 77.

This development took place in many of the Celtic monasteries, and we find them living on into the mediaeval system as houses of Augustinian canons. And Scone became the crowning or inauguration place of Scottish and Pictish kings from Kenneth McAlpin's time onwards. Hence the great importance of the stone.

Inauguration of a chief upon a stone was the usual Celtic practice. It was not confined to Celtic people, but was also Teutonic. In England several of the Saxon kings were inaugurated on a rough stone once in the church of Kingston-on-Thames, but now standing in the town. In Scotland and Ireland several remain. Some have a foot-shaped hollow provided for the new ruler to place his foot as he stood for the ceremony. This included the taking of an oath, the delivery of a sword and a white rod, with possibly a crown or helmet. Sometimes the chief sat on the stone. After this, in Celtic Scotland, there seems to have been a religious ceremony carried out by seven bishops or priests. Practice seems to have varied. Usually the inauguration ceremony took place on the Mote Hill outside the church of Scone. One account reads as if the civil ceremony took place between the two parts of the Mass, as in the Pontifical of Archbishop Egbert in the eighth century. But it would seem that the stone was civil rather than ecclesiastical in its main uses, and that it belonged to a ceremony that was very closely connected with the idea of tribal possession of land. Evidence from seals has been produced which suggests that the stone was enclosed in a chair much as it is at present. The Scone stone was not brought from a great distance, but probably quarried from the Sidlaw Hills not far away.

Going back to the story of King Aidan being consecrated by S. Columba in A.D. 574, we note that there was no anointing. But there was laying of hands which was the equivalent of it. The Scottish kings were not anointed or crowned in the strict sense until it was used by papal authority at the coronation of David II in 1331. Of the service then used we know nothing.

For more information, see *Scottish Coronations*, by John, 3rd Marquess of Bute, Paisley, 1902, and *Four Scottish Coronation Services*, by the late Dr. James Cooper, in a special issue of the *Transactions of the Aberdeen and Glasgow Ecclesiological Societies*, Aberdeen, 1902.

THE SAXON CORONATIONS AT KINGSTON-ON-THAMES

IN Saxon times Kingston was a place of great importance, and the following Saxon kings were crowned there:

Edward the Elder	A.D. 902
Athelstane	A.D. 924
Edmund	A.D. 940
Edred	A.D. 946
Edwy	A.D. 955
[Edgar the Pacific was crowned at Bath by S. Dunstan in A.D. 973]	
Edward the Martyr	A.D. 975
Ethelred the Unready	A.D. 979

Edward the Confessor was crowned at Winchester in 1048, and since then all the kings have been crowned at Westminster.

The service used in the earlier Kingston coronations was possibly the first form, that in the Pontifical of Archbishop Egbert.

There is reason to believe that the Second Order, so-called, was used for the coronation of Edgar at Bath in 973 and no doubt subsequently. We possess a contemporary account of the Bath ceremony, but have no documentary evidence about the Kingston services.

The parish church of All Saints, Kingston-on-Thames, is a large building of many periods. Close beside the south-east corner of it there was a separate church or chapel of S. Mary. Enlargement of the church made the chapel a sort of outer aisle. This chapel collapsed in 1730, and later illustrations then show it as if separate from the church. Excavations have disclosed its foundations south and east of the south transept. It is not certain whether this chapel or the church of All Saints was the place of coronation. But on its destruction in 1730 a rough block of quartzite, traditionally said to be the coronation stone of the Saxon kings, was removed from the chapel and set up outside the Guildhall. Latterly it was moved to more than one place in the street near the Market Place. It is now in an enclosure opposite the Guildhall. It is considered doubtful if the stone is really what it has been assumed to be.

Those interested in these Kingston coronations will find the whole subject dealt with in 'The Site of the Saxon Church at Kingston,' by G. H. Freeman, in *Surrey Archaeological Collections*, Vol. xxxv.

THE HEALING POWER

A N important but little explored aspect of the anointing is its relation to the healing power. The supernormal healing power is one of the spiritual gifts. As a rule the possessor has it independently of any action by the Church. The Church has it, of course, corporately, and can exercise it through the ministry. Her bishops and priests can bless holy oil which others including lay people of both sexes can afterwards administer, and it is possible for a 'thaumaturgos' or wonder worker[1]—that is to say, one with the gift—of either sex, to consecrate it.

How far can the gift be stimulated by unction? Quite possibly to some extent. Thus it seems likely that the healing power with which some kings and queens have been endowed may well have been stimulated and strengthened by the anointing.

Cases of healing apart from normal means are exciting much greater interest to-day than used to be the case. And many who would have talked about superstition not so very long ago, will now be prepared to admit that there must have been something in the case of Queen Anne to make it worth while to add to the Prayer Book the special form 'At the Healing' which we find in so many Prayer Books printed in her reign, and to some extent soon afterwards. Several sovereigns gave a considerable amount of time and trouble in using the

[1] See Puller, *The Anointing of the Sick.*

power. There were fixed times for doing it. The patients were subject to careful inquiry, and under some kings there was a system of tickets or tokens in the form of medals which were a check at the time and could be worn afterwards. The number of people was so great that the strain on the king must have been very exhausting, and the results must often have been far from satisfactory. Yet it seems clear that if the results had always been negative, the thing could not have gone on.

We know enough now to realize that there is a great deal we do not know. To what extent can the gift be hereditary? If this be true, even to a limited degree, it may well be that the coronation anointing helps it to develop. But experience shows that even the people with the strongest healing power are often up against some forces that they cannot overcome. Instead of recognizing this, there is the constant risk that a failure we do not understand may provoke a denial of the reality of the power.

There is also the fact that some people with the power have a special aptitude for treating certain classes of cases, but not perhaps others. We find the tradition of royal power being able to cure scrofula both ancient and constant, so much that scrofula used to be called the King's Evil.

There is no space, and this book is not the place to attempt anything approaching an adequate discussion of this deep and far-reaching subject.

THE ECCLESIASTICAL POWER OF THE QUEEN REGNANT

QUESTIONS have at times been asked about giving so much ecclesiastical power to a Queen, and vesting her in the sacred vestments. The answer is that nothing here goes beyond what was frequently practised of old in the case of deaconesses and certain heads of religious orders and of houses of secular canonesses. The deaconess wore the stole and took the chalice from the altar herself: and certain abbesses and prioresses had ecclesiastical jurisdiction and appointed to livings. They carried croziers and sometimes (as with secular canonesses) wore albes, surplices, or rochets. These things have been strangely forgotten: for it was only in 1919 that the Committee appointed by Archbishop Davidson on the Ministry of Women printed a full account of the part women have taken in the services of the Church. Nothing given in the case of a Queen Regnant exceeds these powers. It ought not to be necessary to reiterate that the Sovereign is not a priest.